The LQ³
A New Paradigm in 21st Century Leader Decision Making

Educators Edition

GEORGE W. RIDEOUT, D.B.A.

JANE BRUSH LILLESTOL, Ph.D.

Dedication

This book is dedicated to everyone who believes in lifelong learning.

Acknowledgments

The authors would like to acknowledge our friend and talented editor Mary Ellen Carew for helping us across the finish line and making this book reality.

Thanks, M.E.

Contents

Foreword

Decision making is important for everyone, especially given the challenges we face in the twenty-first century. Technology and the global business environment add fuel to this fire, creating an environment of rapid change and widespread circulation of information. We can hear about news instantly, regardless of location via smartphones and tablets linking us to the information superhighway. Nearly everyone owns, or knows someone who owns, at least one of these devices. We question how we could survive without access to so much data!

The richness of technology and the global economy is a double-edged sword. Individuals have the luxury of using this easy access to information to help in decision making. This easily creates overload, however, in which a person must identify only the most valuable data from this vast sea of information and ignore the rest. Overcoming this challenge of twenty-first century decision making requires a new mindset. We can no longer consider only what is in our personal best interest or decide only in the 'now.' We must consider the ramifications or spill-over of our decisions and think for the future. These in turn require us to consider our biases and expand our vision of what makes a good decision.

Milton Friedman once said there is no free lunch. In today's society, there is no free lunch especially when it comes to decision making.

Whatever the decision, the spill-over may be dramatic. The social media craze provides a good example of this. Every day we run into the term *going viral*. An apparently simple, well thought out decision may cause a chain reaction of events, ultimately leading to a more complex decision.

The recent Netflix debacle reinforces this point. Netflix leaders decided to implement changes to their rental programs, including increasing fees, and establishing a separate entity to manage their DVD rental business. The results were disastrous and led to a mass exodus of reportedly 800,000 subscribers! Inevitably, Netflix leaders amended their decision and did not split the company. They are now trying to recover from their decision. Clearly, Netflix leaders considered only what was in their best interest. Netflix leaders could have formulated a decision advantageous to all parties. If Netflix leadership had considered the culture of their customer base and, perhaps more important, the change forces taking place in the video rental market, including anticipated change resulting from their decision, the debacle may not have happened.

People must now look beyond their personal ego to consider culture and change when making a decision. Hot buttons such as culture and how to account for change are now important constructs in the decision-making process. "How will my decision influence others?" "What changes could my decision cause?" "Who is my audience?" "Am I isolating myself by my decision?" Questions like these are important to the decision-making process. In addition, we must consider our *self* and personal comfort level. Our emotional intelligence or intra-personal skills heighten the complexity of making a decision. Ultimately, if we do not feel comfortable in our own skin, we cannot fully appreciate and account for bias. We will limit our ability to gauge culture and change issues.

The unbiased leader decision-making model, LQ^3, is the result of these realizations. The LQ^3 offers a unique perspective, providing a visualization of the new twenty-first century decision-making process, showing the inter-relationship of emotional, cultural, and change leadership intelligence. The model is a road map for heightened awareness, which creates an opportunity for each of us to analyze our own psyche, how we formulate a decision, and how we can temper our biases. Perhaps more important, the LQ^3 is an easy to understand template for educators to bring the decision-making message into the classroom.

I am sure you will agree giving our students the tools to function at their highest potential is vital to society's future success. This booklet is for anyone interested in learning more about decision making. The booklet provides a scholarly paper outlining the basis for LQ^3 and a sample case study to create classroom dialogue. Additionally, readers have an opportunity to download two PowerPoint presentations, and the case study to facilitate classroom teaching. As you read this booklet, I hope you gain increased appreciation for the importance of decision making in the new millennium.

Technology and the integration of society have created a tremendous opportunity for each of us to make a difference and leave our mark on the world. I challenge you to develop your LQ^3!

—George Rideout

Occasionally, as an educator, you may have the great fortune to encounter a student who challenges your thinking and, in the process, becomes both a catalyst and collaborator. Such is the case with my partnership with George Rideout. From the first day of our first class together, it was clear George was exceptional in so many ways. Not content with simply meeting the course requirements, George was full of "what ifs?" He gave a whole new meaning to the term *paradigm shift*.

With my origins in family social science, my focus was on the impact of family systems, and how each of us has been shaped in large part by others in our inner circle. Family, in the broadest terms, encompassed individuals with whom we shared our innermost dreams, desires and life experiences. What made us unique? Where did our strengths come from? What did "intelligence" mean? Gardner's work on multiple intelligences in the 1980s opened my eyes to a brand new perspective, one that resonated strongly with me – an appreciation for the unique talents that lie within each of us.

Building on this was the concept of single, double, and triple loop learning within the context of critical and reflexive thinking. What are common thought patterns? How does one break out of the acceptable and focus on the unfamiliar? What shapes an individual to make a difference in this world, to see through a unique and change-making lens?

And along came George! He rocked my paradigm, and shifted it from an internal, to an external, focus. Instead of looking at change from the perspective of how I, or others, might make it happen, George concentrated on change as the end result, and began to analyze what caused it. Sort of like building a bridge from two different perspectives, we were incredibly fortunate to have the two parts connect.

And what a connection it has become! The LQ^3 Model captures both perspectives and will provide today's visionary leaders with the tools to analyze their unique situations and ultimately discover a groundbreaking solution that will position them on the cutting edge.

—Jane Lillestol

The LQ³
A New Paradigm in 21st Century Leader Decision Making

Educators Edition

1 Research Paper

A new global economy has heightened the demands placed on leaders. Leaders are challenged to react to change faster (Wieand, Birchfield, & Johnson, 2008), making decisions that will influence the long-term direction of their organizations, and the livelihood of their stakeholders (Finkelstein, Whitehead, & Campbell, 2009). Because quality decision making is paramount for success, a clearer understanding of the leader decision-making process may influence outcomes positively.

Bossidy and Charan (2002) saw decisiveness as integral to good decision making, believing the most effective leaders could set aside emotions and make difficult decisions. Drucker (1966) stated that effective leaders made decisions systematically, using a defined process to understand the stressors of decision making and consider each influence when making a decision. This systems approach to decision making supports the notion that effective decision making does not happen in a vacuum but rather is precipitated by an integrated network of stressors occurring internally and externally in the leader's environment.

Senge (2006), using a method developed in the 1960s at MIT called the Beer Game (MIT Forum for Supply Chain Information, 1960), argued most leaders were hindered in their decision making by their own internal thinking process. The game was based upon the production and distribution of one brand of beer. Each of the three players—retailer, wholesaler, and marketing director—was challenged to maximize profit. Outcomes of the Beer Game provided validation of Senge's opinion, showing participants did not think naturally in systems or consider the influence of their decisions. As negative outcomes began to arise, the players reverted to past actions that had been successful rather than applying logic and seeking new solutions.

The literature is rich with data on three forms of leader intelligence: emotional, change, and cultural. The literature does not address, however, the potential links that exist among these forms of leader intelligence or, specifically, how they, working in tandem, may influence a leader's decision-making ability. This knowledge gap has created an opportunity to research the potential links and propose a new leadership model to bridge the knowledge gap and help leaders overcome bias in the decision-making process. Toward this end, an examination will be made of how internal and external systems, in the form of change, stimulate the leadership decision-making process, and how a leader's emotional, cultural, and change leadership intelligence may affect the leader's ability to make a decision.

The literature review will focus on three areas of leader intelligence: (a) emotional intelligence, (b) cultural intelligence, and (c) change leadership intelligence. A new model will then be proposed which is based on the literature findings and grounded in multiple intelligence and systems theories.

The model may assist leaders in reducing potential bias in the decision-making process.

Literature Review

Decision making

Decision making influences every aspect of human life (Finkelstein et al., 2009). Drucker (1966) described decision making in the simplest context as making a judgment. In the business world, how leaders make decisions may define success or failure. Understanding how and why people make decisions, in particular, from a leadership perspective, is an important construct. Decision making studies have roots in the social sciences. The twentieth century is abundant with theories regarding influences on human behavior.

Attribution theory, causal reasoning theory (CRT), social cognitive theory (SCT), and game theory have all contributed to the critical focus of this paper, the reasoning process in leader's decision making. Attribution theory, first proposed by Heider (1958), is the act of attributing a particular cause to an individual's thinking and/or behavior. Weiner (1974) took the concept to another level, developing a theoretical framework for the social sciences. Causal reasoning theory relates to how leaders incorporate prior successes and failures into their decision-making process (McCormick & Martinko, 2004). Social cognitive theory seeks to tie together theories such as attribution and causal reasoning to explain how leaders process decisions using emotions and experiences. Game theory, created by 1920s mathematician John von Neumann (von Neumann, Morgenstern, Rubinstein, & Kuhn, 1944), added a unique flair to the decision-making arena, by suggesting leaders take emotions and irrationality out of the decision-making equation through a logical process. Each theory, although unique, shares common ground in the call for leaders to become cognizant of the internal decision-making process. Without this cognizance, perhaps leaders may face what Drucker (1966) described as "sloppy thinking" (p. 114).

Matzler, Bailom, and Mooradian (2007) described optimal decision making as gut or intuition based, in which leaders primarily used instinct to compose decisions. Ind and Watt (2005) posed a similar argument from a brand marketing perspective, stating that creative judgment based on leader intuition could help organizations create value in the marketplace. Chuang (2007) offered a different perspective based on positive and negative emotions. According to Chuang (2007), research showed a correlation between positive emotions and heightened decision making, suggesting potential bias in the leader decision-making process. Heightened awareness of the role emotions play in the decision making process may aid leaders in managing their emotions to avoid bias in their decision making. The common thread running through each of the preceding arguments is the call for leaders to develop their leader intelligence to enhance decision-making capabilities.

4

A Systems Perspective

Systems are used to describe the integrated connection evident in nearly every aspect of life (Meadows, 2008). Systems exist in many forms, from the simple single cell amoeba to the complex multi-hierarchal organization. Using a business perspective, Johnson, Kast, and Rosenzweig (1964) stated systems appeared within systems, creating a complex network of integration in which each system influenced the others. Systems are believed to be evolutionary (Johnson et al., 1964; Meadows, 2008).

Systems thinking has been studied as far back as the 1600s by scientists such as Newton and, later, Darwin (Johnson et al., 1964). Whereas Newton's systems were grounded on order and stability, social systems are by nature unstable and unpredictable (Kiel & Elliott, 1996). "Chaos theory" is used to describe this social phenomenon. Cause and effect are often difficult to discern. As social scientists work toward gaining credibility for chaos theory, there has been an ongoing effort to identify patterns based upon nonlinear systems. Lorenz (1963), a mathematician and meteorologist credited as the founder of chaos theory, posited that miniscule actions could lead to major change. Lorenz coined the term "butterfly effect," saying the seemingly insignificant movement of a butterfly's wings could affect weather at a far distant location.

The ideology of systems thinking did not begin to take shape until the first half of the twentieth century when von Bertalanffy created general systems theory (GST) (Mulej et al., 2004). GST helped explain the idea of holism or the integrated nature of everything in the world influenced by World War I and World War II (Mulej, & et al., 2004). Since von Bertalanffy's work, systems thinking has permeated academia and scholarly research, providing an explanation of life on earth.

Von Bertalanffy's description of open systems will form the basis for the proposed LQ^3 model. According to Johnson et al. (1964), open systems mean an organism, simple or complex, "maintains a constant state while matter and energy which enter it keep changing" (p. 371). The latter suggests the influence change in external systems can have on the organization and its leadership, lending support for the proposed LQ^3 model.

Leader Bias

Cohen (2008) believed assumptions formed the basis for all decisions. These assumptions created bias in the leader decision-making process. Leader bias, a recipe for ineffectiveness and organizational disaster, is a learned trait leaders can correct (Thiederman, 2004). Solving the bias equation requires leaders to become cognizant of their personal belief system, including subconscious thoughts (Thiederman, 2004). Unless leaders understand what causes them to react and make decisions, bias may continue to exist, skewing the leaders' perceptions and creating misguided decisions.

Krause (2010), using "the BP Gulf oil spill catastrophe" as an example, stated that "Cognitive biases are responsible for all types of errors in judgment, risk assessment, and decision-making" (p. 46). Cognitive bias suggests leaders will make assumptions based on experience and culture exposure (Krause, 2010). These assumptions create a comfortable space in which leaders allow assumptions to dominate their decision making, leading to a false sense of awareness. Krause (2010) and Senge (2006) each used the boiled frog analogy to show the fallacies inherent in cognitive leadership behavior. Leaders, similar to the frog in the pot, will not react until the situation causing a decision places their organization in such peril they are forced to concede. Often the decision comes too late, and the leader and respective organization risk competitive advantage. Senge (2006) cited the United States automotive industry during the 1960s and the emergence of foreign competitors, such as Toyota, as a good example of leader decisions misguided by assumptions. Decisions made by the Big Three automotive leaders caused severe damage to their long-term viability by diminishing valued market-share in the North American markets (Senge, 2006).

Bandura's social cognitive theory helps explain human behavior, including the decision-making process (McCormick & Martinko, 2004). Social cognitions are used to describe the decision-making process as well as the stressors that influence the process (McCormick & Martinko, 2004). These stressors are both internal and external to the leader. Stressors such as competition, stakeholders, and even the ego of the leader may create pressure to change. Leaders may choose either a reactive or a proactive approach to managing these change forces.

Leader Intelligence

Leadership success depends on several factors, including the operating environment and leader intelligence. As a result of his work with both gifted and brain-damaged children, Gardner (1983) created the theory of multiple intelligences (MI) to explain the complexity of human thinking. Initially, Gardner identified seven types of intelligence: linguistic, logical-mathematical, musical, spatial, bodily-kinesthetic, interpersonal, and intrapersonal. Gardner (2000) has since added naturalistic intelligence and is considering a ninth—existential— intelligence. Understanding how multiple leader intelligences work together may have a positive influence on leader success in the organization (Wilson & Mujtaba, 2010).

Fiedler (1981) argued that leader knowledge and skills are important ingredients in leadership success. Shambaugh (2005) agreed, coining the term "integrated leader" (p.15). According to Shambaugh (2005), most leaders eliminate more than 50 percent of their leadership skills because they do not use integrated thinking when making a decision.

Integrated thinking suggests leaders should (a) look at their personal assumptions, (b) weigh their "integrated leadership quotient," and (c) not allow gender to play a role in the decision-making process (Shambaugh, 2005, p. 16). The "integrated leadership quotient" provides gender-based skills

8

assessment for leaders (Shambaugh, 2005, p. 16). Although the Shambaugh (2005) argument focuses on reducing limitations created by allowing gender to play a role in leaders' decision-making, the model supports a call for leaders to develop their leadership intelligence, and become aware of their personal biases which may negatively influence the decision-making process.

Albrecht (2003) identified an organizational intelligence (OI) model integrating multiple forms of human intelligence, occurring in the organization. The model, points to learning that occurs consciously and unconsciously, suggesting that humans learn at more than one level (Stalinski, 2004). These "dimensions of competence," meant for organizational learning, are based on the human psyche, and show how harnessing together multiple intelligences may heighten the learning process (Stalinski, 2004, p. 56).

Gardner's (1983) original "seven domains of multiple intelligences" (Wilson & Mujtaba, 2010, p. 2) included the gray area humans possess that could not be explained easily with formal IQ tests (Conti, 2008), considered by many scholars as the nonacademic intelligences (Kumar, Rose, & Subramaniam, 2008). These ideas posited by Gardner (1983) spawned several more dimensions of intelligence including emotional and cultural because of later work by Goleman (1995) and Albrecht (2006, 2007).

Emotional Intelligence (EQ)

Leader emotional intelligence (EQ) is found in all corners of academia and research. The literature's richness and the intrigue of later EQ studies date from Aristotle's *Nicomachean Ethics*, in which Aristotle linked emotions and intelligence (Aristotle, trans. 1908). In *On Dreams*, Aristotle used as an example of the transmission of heat, wherein transference occurs to adjacent parts, culminating in a return to its origin (Aristotle, as translated by J. I. Beare). Cognitively, this can be understood. Emotions are generated by the actions as well, however, and remain even when we move on to another activity. Today the EQ debates appear to center on a common theme; how EQ influences a leader's performance in the organization, including the leader's decision-making process. A modern definition of EQ is the leader's ability to become cognizant not only of his or her own emotions and moods but also those of other stakeholders in the external environment (George, 2000). George (2000) extended this definition by stating that EQ may promote leadership effectiveness in areas such as decision making and change management.

Scientific evidence shows a link between a person's emotions and moods and cognitive capabilities (Chuang, 2007); EQ may positively or negatively influence the ability to make effective decisions (George, 2000; Goleman, 1995, 1998). A lack of EQ may help explain why some leaders, although highly intelligent, make flawed decisions that severely hinder the livelihood of their organization and its stakeholders (Goleman, 1995). The Socratic "Know thyself" is an important axiom for all leaders seeking EQ, because it demystifies the complexity of EQ, the ability of leaders to recognize and understand their own emotional state (Goleman, 1995). This insight lends credence to Drucker's (1999) statement about how assumptions equal reality. Humans create reality based on closely held beliefs and assumptions, even though most people, including scholars, rarely deconstruct assumptions to determine validity (Drucker, 1999). This further supports the EQ argument in the leadership equation.

Finkelstein et al. (2009) examined how leader decision making may become flawed by leader experience. Research suggests a leader may unknowingly base a decision on the emotion created by an experience (Finkelstein et al., 2009). Finkelstein et al. (2009) described the phenomena as "unconsciously misled" (p. 38). Leader emotions may cloud judgment and create bias in the decision-making process (Chuang, 2007).

Goleman (1998) identified five components of emotional intelligence: (a) self-awareness, (b) self-regulation, (c) motivation, (d) empathy, and (e) social skills. Self-awareness describes the leader's becoming aware of his or her emotions and their influence on others (Goleman, 1998). Self-regulation points to a person's self-control over emotions and motivation to accomplish goals (Goleman, 1998). Empathy implies leaders need to understand the needs of others and acquire the social skills necessary to creating and managing relationships (Goleman, 1998). Each component creates a call for leaders to understand their personal psyche and the makeup of their unconscious and conscious thought processes. Because each component influences the leader at various junctures in the leadership process, there appears to be a correlation between how the leader acts/reacts in the decision-making process and how he or she manages emotions. This influence posits a systems argument.

Cultural Intelligence (CQ)

Cultural intelligence studies became common in the late twentieth century, as academics and business leaders began to realize the importance and influence of culture on the organization. Leaders in the twenty-first century face a unique group of challenges because of the new global economy; culture is at the center of these challenges. How leaders manage cultural differences and, more important, allow cultural biases into their decision-making process may determine the leaders' and organizations' success. Learning to manage these global challenges requires leaders to create organizational cultures with heightened receptivity to change and new ideas.

Cheng (2007) challenged leaders to develop a higher level of thought about cultural acceptance in society. Basing her opinions on the 2007 Virginia Technology tragedy, in which 33 people including the shooter, Seung-Hui Cho, were killed, Cheng posited greater cultural competency could have been the key to prevention; she stressed the importance of managing

12

first impressions. Cultural, linguistic, and social contexts are unique lenses that can aid leaders in sharpening their focus as they attempt to decode messages received from unfamiliar cultures.

Bennis and Nanus (1985) posited effective leaders should knock down walls and eliminate potential biases with the goal of creating a constantly evolving, sponge-like, and open organizational culture. Shambaugh's (2005) integrated thinking approach provides support for Bennis and Nanus' argument, stressing the importance of a leader's recognizing his or her personal biases that may impair sound decision making and impede the development of new ideas and anticipation of future challenges. Kofman (2006) labeled this faith in personal biases *ontological arrogance*, the belief that one's personal experiences are accurate reflections of reality and supersede the reality as seen by others. A quotation from the Talmud was used to reinforce this point: "We do not see things as they are. We see things as we are (p.97)." Rather, Kofman (2006) has suggested leaders should practice *ontological humility*, respecting the views of others as valid and worthy of consideration. Cheng (2007) also used the term *ontological humility* in the context of dealing with cultural diversity.

Building upon the work by Bennis and Nanus (1985), Janssens and Brett (2006) proposed the Fusion Model of Global Team Collaboration to explain the highly integrated operating environment facing organizations in the twenty-first century. The model is based upon the concept of fusion cooking, in which chefs unleash their creativity by fusing together a diverse group of spices and flavors to create new dishes, such as using Italian spices in a Mexican dish. Applying the model to an organizational context, Janssens and Brett (2006) called for leaders to fuse their organizations culturally to take advantage of global opportunities and knowledge. Fusion thinking, although meant for group collaboration on a global scale, may also apply to leader decision making. If leaders fuse or integrate their leader intelligence and adopt an open-minded perspective regarding the decision-making process, the result may be an increase in creativity and heightened awareness, and elimination of biases that could skew effective decision-making.

Change Leadership Intelligence (CLQ)

Landale (2004) defined leadership for the twenty-first century as the ability of leaders to deliver and carry out organizational change. In her analysis of organizational success, Kanter (1984) described change masters as corporate visionaries who were able to create a new organizational culture within an established institution, one which was open and decentralized to allow for increased communication and increased access to resources. Effectively carrying out change requires the development of emotional and spiritual intelligences (Landale, 2004). Change leadership intelligence, instigated by the onslaught of radical change evident in society during the late twentieth century, may be the latest addition to multiple intelligence studies. The new global economy, coupled with extraordinary advances in technology, is forcing leaders to deal with change at a faster pace than ever before (Ferres & Connell, 2004). An understanding of why change happens, the implications of change for the organization, and the importance of aligning leadership thinking and visions may have a profound impact on an organization's success.

Effective organizational leaders are change agents (Arora, 2003). To become a change agent, leaders are challenged to learn about not only themselves and their respective thought processes but also those individuals they influence (Arora, 2003). Unless leaders learn to let go of baggage created by learned assumptions and experiences, they may become incapable of enacting change in themselves and the organization (Arora, 2003).

Duck (2001) identified three areas in which leaders should focus to enact change: (a) strategy, (b) execution, and (c) sensitivity. Strategy implies development of a game plan showing the end result, and execution suggests strategy cannot be enacted without a solid plan of execution (Duck, 2001). Lastly, sensitivity calls for leaders to perform an evaluation of self and their organization, both emotionally and behaviorally. Duck's (2001) vision is in alignment with a common theme running throughout this paper—the importance of successful leaders becoming in tune with their environments, including their inner selves.

A New Model - LQ³

The LQ³ model (see *Figure 1*), using a systems perspective, builds on prior multiple intelligence research to provide a roadmap explaining the leader decision-making process. LQ³ represents a unique meshing of intelligence research by Fiedler (1981), Gardner (1983), Goleman (1995, 1998), and Shambaugh (2005) with social cognitive, decision-making, and systems theorists such as Heider (1958), Weiner (1974), Meadows (2008), and von Neumann et al. (1944). Using this foundation, the model postulates a new synthesis of the leader decision-making process, linking emotional, cultural, and change leadership intelligences with internal and external systems and change forces. Further, the model suggests the influence of leader bias in the decision-making process and how, by developing emotional, cultural, and change leadership intelligences, leaders may reduce bias and enhance decision making.

The diagram of LQ³ shows how external and internal systems react upon and within the leader to the benefit of his/her organization. The leader identifies external change stressors (indicated by stars on the left side of Figure 1), considers them in light of the leader's own internal stressors (the question marks on the right side of Figure 1), and identifies the best course of action. The model shows linkages between emotional, cultural, and change leadership intelligence, which encourages leaders to consider all possible biases created by these intelligences. The model also demonstrates that LQ³ learning is ongoing. Making unbiased decisions enhances leaders' intelligence and creates a reinforcing feedback loop. The model opens the door to future study by allowing researchers to visualize the intelligence linkages along with the influence of internal and external systems.

Assessing implementation of the LQ^3 model requires syncing the processes evident in the model with the leader psyche. A viable framework may be found using Bloom's Taxonomy. Bloom, Engelhart, Furst, Hill, and Krathwohl (1956) identified six areas of intellectual capability, each building on the other to suggest a cognitive learning process, and that learning becomes more complex with learner cognition. The areas include: (1) knowledge, (2) comprehension, (3) application, (4) analysis, (5) synthesis, and (6) evaluation (Bloom et al., 1956). The LQ^3 suggests a similar process in a leader decision-making context. Applying this foundation, a proposed template for assessing model implementation is offered in Appendix A. Educators may find the template suitable for case study evaluation in the classroom. Appendix B includes a list of well-known tested emotional and cultural intelligence assessments.

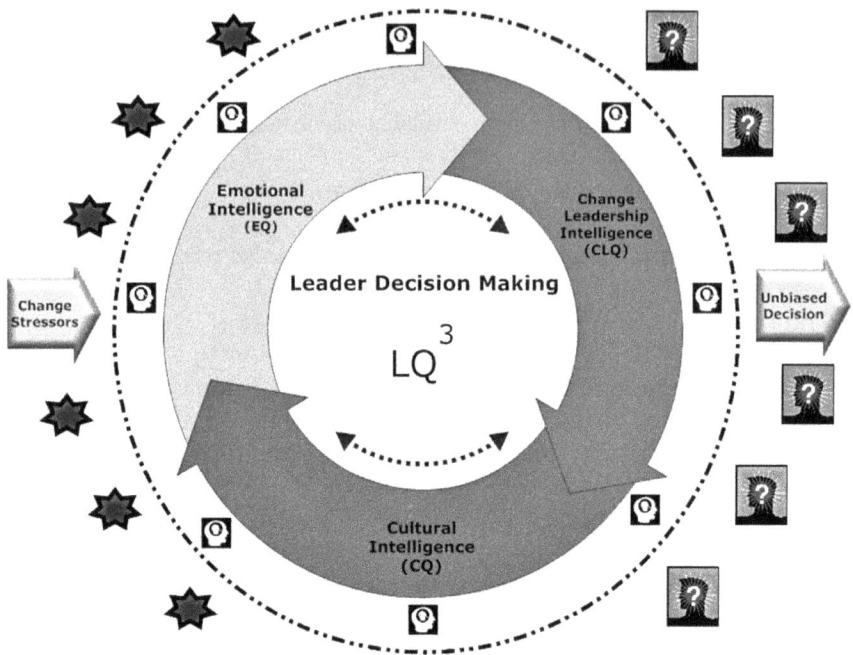

Figure 1. The Unbiased Leader Decision Making Model

Conclusions

Blake and McCanse (1991) stated leaders use assumptions to make business decisions. These assumptions create a reality for leaders and become silent predators, controlling leader behavior behind the scenes (Blake & McCanse, 1991). James (1996) noted one's perspective might easily become distorted if assumptions are considered realities. According to Blake and McCanse (1991), leaders can, through increased awareness, recognize and change their assumptions, and, ultimately, their behavior.

The Blake and McCanse (1991) proposal supports the arguments made throughout this paper; the need for leaders to become in tune with their inner selves in order to positively influence their decision-making processes. Enhancing one's multiple intelligences—emotional, cultural, and change leadership, each working as autonomous but integrated systems—can positively influence behavior behind the psychic curtain of the human mind. Perhaps Socrates was right when he coined "know thyself," because clearly, removing bias from the leader decision-making process begins with the leader. The proposed LQ^3 model may be used by leaders to visually understand these linkages and cement a new path to effective, unbiased, decision making.

2 Case Study

Implementing LQ^3 in the classroom requires an assessment tool to bridge the gap between theory and application. A case study provides an appropriate format. In the case study, students apply the decision-making model to a fictitious business situation. Case discussion questions focus on encouraging dialogue, such as how the leader in the case scenario exhibits high or low emotional, cultural, and change leadership intelligence, and how the leader may enhance the intelligences to make unbiased decisions. The case study may help student cognitive ability to make unbiased decisions and more important become effective leaders beyond college and in life.

The LQ^3

The LQ^3 model (see *Figure 1*), using a systems perspective, builds on prior multiple intelligence research to provide a roadmap explaining the leader decision-making process. LQ^3 represents a unique meshing of intelligence research by Fiedler (1981), Gardner (1983), Goleman (1995, 1998), and Shambaugh (2005) with social cognitive, decision-making, and systems theorists such as Heider (1958), Weiner (1974), Meadows (2008), and von Neumann et al. (1944). Using this foundation, the model postulates a new synthesis of the leader decision-making process, linking emotional, cultural, and change leadership intelligences with internal and external systems, and change forces. Further, the model suggests the influence of leader bias in the decision-making process and how developing emotional, cultural, and change leadership intelligences leaders may reduce bias and enhance decision making.

The diagram of LQ^3 shows how external and internal systems react upon and within the leader to the benefit of his/her organization. The leader identifies external change stressors (indicated by stars on the left side of Figure 1), considers them in light of the leader's own internal stressors (the question marks on the right side of Figure 1), and identifies the best course of action. The model shows linkages between emotional, cultural, and change leadership intelligence, which encourages leaders to consider all possible biases created by these intelligences. The model also demonstrates that LQ^3 learning is ongoing. Making unbiased decisions enhances leaders' intelligence and creates a reinforcing feedback loop. The model opens the door to future study by allowing researchers to visualize the intelligence linkages along with the influence of internal and external systems.

Sample Company Overview

[Author's note: These events are based on actual trends and market forces, but the authors have not used the names of real people, companies, or locations. There is no "Southeast New England Shoe Company" in Gardiner, Maine, and no Glidden family who own and operate it. Except for cited data, the case is fictional, and is not representative of any person or entity.] The fictional Southeast New England Shoe Company is a 125 year-old family-owned footwear manufacturer based in Gardiner, Maine. The Glidden family patriarch, Ralph Glidden, founded the company. Today, CEO and President Donald Glidden, the great-grandson of founder Ralph Glidden, operates the company. Southeast manufactures a variety of footwear, including men's, ladies', and children's athletic, casual, and dress. The company operates three factories in Gardiner, Richmond, and Hallowell, Maine. The Gardiner factory currently employs 320 people; Richmond, 240; and Hallowell, 220. Southeast is considered the largest employer in each locale.

Industry Overview

United States shoe manufacturing is in decline, and research suggests 95 percent of all shoes sold in the U.S. are imported from countries such as China and Vietnam (Hoovers, 2011). As most companies shift from manufacturing to design and move production offshore, a report by IBISWorld (2011) states "this industry has one foot in the grave" (p. 4). Major U.S. shoe brands such as Nike and Timberland outsource their shoe production to offshore locations (Hoovers, 2011). Small, regionalized manufacturers who specialize in lines such as high priced men's footwear are the last bastion of domestic manufacturing (Hoovers, 2011).

Growth opportunities in the shoe industry center on market niches and finding unique ways to harness technology to reach consumers. Using the Internet, identifying potential markets outside the United States and extending shoe brands to include other apparel represent viable opportunities in the marketplace (Hoovers, 2011). Focusing on high-end shoes could provide a much needed niche for the remaining U.S. shoe manufacturers because foreign markets often lack access to expensive raw materials readily available in the United States (IBISWorld, 2011). Research suggests imports will continue gaining traction on domestic products, causing U.S. manufacturers to identify ways to cut costs and heighten efficiencies (IBISWorld, 2011).

Local Market Overview

The local Maine economy is weak, and unemployment is significantly above the national average at nearly 13 percent. The economy has been lagging behind national averages for more than a decade. The manufacturing base is dwindling, and most companies have moved operations outside the state or consolidated with other non-Maine based manufacturers to create economies of scale. The shoe industry, a staple in the Maine economy since the late eighteenth century, is nearly nonexistent. Empty buildings, once busy factories, dot the landscape throughout out shoe towns across Maine. Significant change has taken place during the last 30 years. See Appendix D for significant events influencing the local economy and Southeast Shoe during the last 30 years.

Southeast CEO Bio

Southeast CEO Donald Glidden is 48. He was born and raised in the small central Maine city of Gardiner and attended local schools including the University of Maine, where he graduated with a bachelor's degree in business administration. Growing up in Maine isolated Donald from much of the world. Other than vacations and the occasional business trip, Donald does not stray far from Maine and his hometown.

Donald is married to Mary, the daughter of Joe Lineman, another prominent business owner in the community. Donald and Mary have three children, Donald Jr. (10), Isabelle (8), and Ralph (4). Donald is known by friends and employees as a kind, outgoing man who believes in family and community. He is a community leader, serves on various local boards, including the Chamber of Commerce, and is a deacon at his church.

Although Donald and his father are close, Donald's grandfather was the greatest influence on his life. Donald was mentored by his grandfather, Charles Glidden. Charles Glidden was a boisterous, old-school man who, like Donald, loved his community and making shoes. Donald has fond memories of his grandfather teaching him the ropes about fishing and how to cut shoes. Donald learned quickly as a youngster that dreams of becoming an astronaut or famous baseball player were far-fetched fantasy and that his place was in the family business. Donald tries to instill the values taught to him in his children, but often wonders what kind of world will exist when his children grow up. The world is changing quickly, and the good life may be gone forever.

Current Situation

Sales for Southeast Shoe totaled $27,700,000 last year, down 16% from the previous year. Sales have declined significantly over the past 10 years, dropping nearly 67% during this period. The most significant decline coincided with the economic slowdown, which began five years ago. This period represented a 52% reduction in sales revenue and the first time the company has lost money. To endure the decline in sales, the company was forced to lay off nearly a quarter of its employees. The latest round of layoffs was the most dramatic, totaling 15% because Southeast leadership exhausted other means to cut overhead. Prior to this, Southeast had been viewed as a staple in the Gardiner, Richmond, and Hallowell communities over its 125-year history, having never endured layoffs. Several generations of locals have worked in the Southeast factories, and the company is known for a culture of family and long-term secure employment. Current CEO Donald Glidden is uneasy about what the future holds for Southeast and knows that drastic measures must be taken to ensure the company remains a viable entity.

The Decision

Southeast CEO Donald Glidden is pondering the next course of action for his company. CEO Glidden knows if revenue does not improve, the company will be forced to consider alternatives because the company cannot continue bleeding cash. If Donald had not tapped financial reserves, the employee layoffs would have been significantly higher. Trusted advisors and family friends have offered advice on how to move forward. Donald has narrowed the alternatives, removing any idea of selling the company off the table:

a) Move some or all of production offshore to reduce production costs, take advantage of tax incentives, and help company increase competitiveness;

b) Retool plants to focus on more lucrative products; and

c) Idle one or more plants until markets turn around

Donald wonders if he decides to move the company offshore, how he will explain this to his workforce. How will he explain this to his father? What would his grandfather think if he were still alive? How will Donald show his children that values are more important than money? How will he explain to his workers that he is taking their jobs and moving them to another country? Donald worries about establishing new relationships. He will have to become acquainted with new markets. Donald has spent his entire career and life in Maine. How will he step outside his comfort zone?

If he decides to retool the plants to focus on more lucrative products, where will Southeast secure the funding? The local banks where Southeast has long-time relationships cannot loan more money as they are struggling to survive. Securing funding will require establishing new banking relationships or perhaps merging with another manufacturer.

The final option means more employee layoffs. Does idling one or more plants mean the company is accepting defeat? Donald wonders if this solution is only a temporary fix to a larger problem. Will Southeast ever be able to re-open the plants? How will Donald make everyone feel good about this decision and maintain employee morale?

Donald does not like any of the options. He often wonders why things can't go back to normal, as they used to be when decisions were easy. Everything seemed to work out just fine. The company was successful. Good secure jobs were provided for many people. These people are Donald's friends, many of whom he has known his entire life. Why is this happening? Donald knows the livelihood of the company rests in his hands, and he must make good decisions not influenced by his emotions.

Discussion Questions

1. Using the LQ^3 model (see *Figure 1*) as a guide, identify the change stressors creating the decision-making process for Donald.

2. Using the definitions provided in Appendix C, how do change leadership, cultural, and emotional intelligence play a role in Donald's decision-making process?

3. Do you think Donald has high or low change leadership, cultural, and emotional intelligence? Why?

4. What biases are evident in Donald's decision-making process, and can you explain the relationship between the intelligences?

5. How do you think Donald's decision-making capabilities are enhanced or hindered by his intelligences?

6. What could Donald do to enhance his intelligences and decision-making capabilities?

References

Albrecht, K. (2003). *The power of minds at work: Organizational intelligence in action.* New York, NY: American Management Association (AMACOM).

Albrecht, K. (2006). *Social intelligence: The new science of success.* San Francisco, CA: Jossey-Bass.

Albrecht, K. (2007). *Practical intelligence: The art and science of common sense.* New York, NY: Jossey-Bass.

Aristotle. (350 B.C.E./1908). *Nicomachean ethics* (W. D. Ross, Trans.). Oxford, UK: Clarendon Press.

Aristotle. (350 B.C.E.). On dreams (J. I. Beare, Trans.). Retrieved from http://classics.mit.edu/Aristotle/dreams.html

Arora, N. (2003). *Theory zyx of successful change management: A definitive practical guide to reach the next level.* Los Angeles, CA: L. A. Press.

Bennis, W., & Nanus, B. (1985). *Leaders: The strategies for taking charge.* New York, NY: Harper & Row Publishers.

Blake, R. R., & McCanse, A. A. (1991). *Leadership dilemmas: Grid solutions.* Houston, TX: Gulf Publishing Company.

Bloom, B.S. (Ed.), Engelhart, M.D., Furst, E.J., Hill, W.H., & Krathwohl, D.R. (1956). *Taxonomy of educational objectives: Handbook I: Cognitive domain.* New York, NY: David McKay.

Bossidy, L., & Charan, R. (2002). *Execution: The discipline of getting things done.*
New York, NY: Crown Business.

Cheng, L. R. L. (2007). Cultural intelligence (CQ): A quest for cultural
competence. *Communication Disorders Quarterly, 29*(1), 36. doi:
10.1177/1525740108314860

Chuang, S.-C. (2007). Sadder but wiser or happier and smarter? A
Demonstration of judgment and decision making. Available from *The
Journal of Psychology, 141*(1): 63-76.

Cohen, W. A. (2008). *A class with Drucker.* New York, NY: American
Management Association (AMACOM).

Conti, H. (2008). Multiple intelligences. *Multiple Intelligences -- Research Starters
Education* 1-1. Retrieved from
http://search.ebscohost.com/login.aspx?direct=true&db=e0h&AN
=27577924&site=ehost-live

Drucker, P. F. (1966). *The effective executive.* New York, NY: Harper Collins.

Drucker, P. F. (1999). *Management challenges for the 21st century.* New York, NY:
Harper Business.

Duck, J. D. (2001). *The change monster: The human forces that fuel or foil corporate
transformation & change.* New York, NY: Crown Business.

Earley, P. C., & Mosakowski, E. (2004). Cultural intelligence. *Harvard Business
Review, 82*(10), 139.

Ferres, N., & Connell, J. (2004). Emotional intelligence in leaders: an antidote for cynicism towards change? *Strategic Change, 13*(2), 61. doi: 10.1002/jsc.665

Fiedler, F. E. (1981). Leadership Effectiveness: Emergent leadership what makes the leader effective? Situational factors determining the role of intelligence and experience in leadership performance. *The American Behavioral Scientist (pre-1986), 24*(5), 619. Retrieved from http://search.proquest.com/docview/194634966?accountid=35812

Finkelstein, S., Whitehead, J., & Campbell, A. (2009). The illusion of smart decision making: The past is not prologue. *The Journal of Business Strategy, 30*(6), 36. doi: 10.1108/02756660911003103

Gardner, H.E. (1983). *Frames of mind: The theory of multiple intelligences.* New York, NY: Perseus/Basic

Gardner, H.E. (2000). *Intelligence reframed: Multiple intelligences for the 21st century.* New York, NY: Basic

George, J. M. (2000). Emotions and leadership: The role of emotional intelligence. *Human Relations, 53*(8), 1027. Retrieved from http://proquest.umi.com/pqdweb?did=84030067&Fmt=7&clientId =13118&RQT=309&VName=PQD

Goleman, D. (1995). *Emotional intelligence: Why it can matter more than IQ.* New York, NY: Bantam Books.

Goleman, D. (1998). What makes a leader? *Harvard Business Review, 76*(6), 93-102. Retrieved from http://search.ebscohost.com/login.aspx?direct=true&db=bth&AN=1246794&site=ehost-live

Heider, F. (1958). *The psychology of interpersonal relations.* New York, NY: John Wiley & Sons.

Hoovers. (2011). Industry profile: Footwear manufacturing. http://www.hoovers.com/industry/footwear-manufacturing/1164-1.html

IBISWorld. (2011). Shoe and footwear manufacturing in the US. http://www.ibisworld.com/industry/default.aspx?indid=369

Ind, N., & Watt, C. (2006). Brands and breakthroughs: How brands help focus creative decision making. *Journal of Brand Management, 13*(4/5), 330. Retrieved from http://proquest.umi.com/pqdweb?did=1077563971&Fmt=7&clientId=13118&RQT=309&VName=PQD

James, J. (1996). *Thinking in the future tense: A workout for the mind.* New York, NY: Touchstone.

Janssens, M., & Brett, J. M. (2006). Cultural intelligence in global teams: A fusion model of collaboration. *Group & Organization Management, 31*(1), 124. doi: 10.1177/1059601105275268

Johnson, R. A., Kast, F. E., & Rosenzweig, J. E. (1964). Systems theory and

    management. *Management Science, 10*(2), 367-384. Retrieved from

    http://search.ebscohost.com/login.aspx?direct=true&db=bth&AN

    =7439987&site=ehost-live

Kanter, (1983). *The change masters: Innovations for productivity in corporate America.*

    New York, NY: Simon & Schuster.

Kiel, L.D. & Elliott, R. Eds. (1997). *Chaos theory in the social sciences: Foundations*

    and applications. Ann Arbor, MI: University of Michigan Press.

Kofman, F. (2006). *Conscious business – how to build value through values.* Boulder,

    CO: Sounds True.

Krause, T. (2010). High-reliability performance: Cognitive biases undermine

    decision making. *ISHN, 44*(9), 46. Retrieved from

    http://search.proquest.com/docview/751609443?accountid=35812

Kumar, N., Rose, R. C., & Subramaniam. (2008). The bond between

    intelligences: Cultural, emotional, and social. *Performance Improvement,*

    47(10), 42. doi: 10.1002/pfi.20039

Landale, A. (2004). Being a leader of change. *The British Journal of Administrative*

    Management, 18. Retrieved from

    http://search.proquest.com/docview/224615306?accountid=35812

Lorenz, E.N. (1963). Deterministic non-periodic flow. *Journal of the Atmosphere Sciences.* 20:130-141. Retrieved from

http://journals.ametsoc.org/doi/abs/10.1175/1520-0469(1963)020%3C0130:DNF%3E2.0.CO;2

Matzler, K., Bailom, F., & Mooradian, T. A. (2007). Intuitive decision making. *MIT Sloan Management Review, 49*(1), 13. Retrieved from http://proquest.umi.com/pqdweb?did=1360145901&Fmt=7&clientId=13118&RQT=309&VName=PQD

McCormick, M. J., & Martinko, M. J. (2004). Identifying leader social cognitions: Integrating the causal reasoning perspective into social cognitive theory. *Journal of Leadership & Organizational Studies, 10*(4), 2. Retrieved from

http://search.proquest.com/docview/203140320?accountid=35812

Meadows, D. H. (2008). *Thinking in systems: A primer.* White River Junction, VT: Chelsea Green Publishing.

MIT Forum for Supply Chain Information. (1960). *Beer Game,* retrieved from http://supplychain.mit.edu/games/beer-game

Mulej, M., Potocan, V., Zenko, Z., Kajzer, S., Ursic, D., Knez-Riedl, J., Lynn, M. & Ovsenik, J. (2004). How to restore Bertalanffian systems thinking. *Kybernetes, 33*(1), 48. Retrieved from http://proquest.umi.com/pqdweb?did=617525371&Fmt=7&clientId=13118&RQT=309&VName=PQD

Rideout, G. W. (2011). *Change leadership intelligence (CLQ): A definition*. Paper presented at the Academic Forum Annual Conference, Fort Lauderdale, FL.

Rideout, G. W., & Lillestol, J. B. (2011). *The LQ³: Unlocking unbiased leader decision making*. Paper presented at the Association of Leadership Educators (ALE) Annual Conference, Denver, CO.

Senge, P. M. (2006). *The fifth discipline: the art and practice of a learning organization*. New York, NY: Doubleday.

Shambaugh, R. L. (2005). The integrated leader. *Leader to Leader, 2005*(36), 15. Retrieved from http://proquest.umi.com/pqdweb?did=810255291&Fmt=7&clientId=13118&RQT=309&VName=PQD

Stalinski, S. (2004). Organizational intelligence: A systems perspective. *Organization Development Journal, 22*(2), 55. Retrieved from http://search.proquest.com/docview/198002795?accountid=35812

Thiederman, S. (2004). The vision renewal process: How to achieve bias-free leadership. *The Journal for Quality and Participation, 27*(4), 4. Retrieved from http://search.proquest.com/docview/219118618?accountid=35812

Von Neumann, J., Morgenstern, O., Rubinstein, A. & Kuhn, H.W. (1944). *Theory of games and economic behavior*. Princeton, NJ, Princeton University Press.

Weiner, B. (1974). *Achievement motivation and attribution theory.* Morristown, NJ: Attribution Press.

Wieand, P., Birchfield, J., & Johnson, M., III. (2008). The new leadership challenge: Removing the emotional barriers to sustainable performance in a flat world. *Ivey Business Journal Online.* Retrieved from http://proquest.umi.com/pqdweb?did=1562515041&Fmt=7&clientId=13118&RQT=309&VName=PQD

Wilson, S. D., & Mujtaba, B. G. (2010). The relationship between leadership and multiple intelligences with the 21st century's higher education faculty. *The Journal of Applied Business and Economics, 11*(3), 106. Retrieved from http://search.proquest.com/docview/816195150?accountid=35812

Appendix A

LQ^3 Model—Case Study Application

Level of Learning	Max. Points	Earned Points	Comments
Identified change stressors	5		
Identified personal biases	5		
Identified three intelligences	5		
Summarized inter-relationships among intelligences	10		
Analyzed inter-relationships among intelligences	15		
Evaluated inter-relationships among intelligences	20		
Created new knowledge leading to an unbiased decision	40		
Total Score:	**100**		

References

Anderson, L.W. & Krathwohl, D.R. (Eds.) (2001). *A taxonomy for Learning, teaching, and   assessing: A revision of Bloom's taxonomy of educational objectives.* New York, NY: Addison Wesley Longman.

Bloom, B.S. (Ed.), Engelhart, M.D., Furst, E.J., Hill, W.H., & Krathwohl, D.R. (1956). *Taxonomy of educational objectives: Handbook I: Cognitive domain.* New York, NY: David McKay.

Appendix B

Assessment Tool Bibliography

Bar-On, R. (1997). *Emotional Quotient Inventory (EQ-i).* **Toronto, Canada: Multi-Health Systems.** The Emotional Quotient Inventory (EQ-i) is a 133 question five-part Likert-scale instrument measuring 15 skills related to human emotions. The questions are further separated into five specific areas including intrapersonal, interpersonal, adaptability, general mood, and stress management. The assessment helps participants identify areas of weakness and conversely helps leverage areas of strength. EQ-i resulted from research by Dr. Reuven Bar-On, and nearly two decades of study, including pilots conducted in six countries. The assessment takes 30 minutes to complete, and uses a normative baseline of almost 4000 subjects to gauge participant responses as below average, average, or above average. Regarded by the scientific community for merit, the EQ-i is a popular and well accepted test of emotional intelligence.

Publisher Contact Info

Multi Health Systems, Inc.

Web Site: www.mhs.com

Email: customerservice@mhs.com

For research: r&d@mhs.com

Phone (Canada):   1-800-268-6011

Phone (USA):   1-800-456-3003

Phone (Intl.):   +1-416-492-2627

Mayer, J., Salovey, P., & Caruso, D. (2002). Mayer-Salovey-Caruso Emotional Intelligence Test: User's manual. Toronto, Canada: Multi-Health Systems. The Mayer-Salovey-Caruso Emotional Intelligence Test (MSCEIT) is an ability-based test designed to measure the four branches of the EI model of Mayer and Salovey. MSCEIT was developed from an intelligence-testing tradition formed by the emerging scientific understanding of emotions and their function and from the first published ability measure specifically intended to assess emotional intelligence, namely Multifactor Emotional Intelligence Scale (MEIS). MSCEIT consists of 141 items and takes 30-45 minutes to complete. MSCEIT provides 15 main scores: Total EI score, two Area scores, four Branch scores, and eight Task scores. In addition to these 15 scores, there are three Supplemental scores (Mayer, Salovey, & Caruso, 2002).

Publisher Contact Info
Multi Health Systems, Inc.
Web Site: www.mhs.com
Email: customerservice@mhs.com
For research: r&d@mhs.com

Phone (Canada):   1-800-268-6011
Phone (USA):   1-800-456-3003
Phone (Intl.):   +1-416-492-2627

Van Dyne, L. (2005). Michigan State University. Cultural Intelligence Center. A 20-item, Four Factor Cultural Intelligence Scale (CQS) includes emphases on strategy, knowledge, motivation, and behavior. Use of this scale granted to academic researchers for research purposes only. For information on using the scale for purposes other than academic research (e.g., consultants and non-academic organizations), please send an email to cquery@culturalq.com

Appendix C

Case Study Definitions

For this case study, the following definitions will be used to guide dialogue:

- **Change Leadership Intelligence:** "…an individual's ability to embrace, identify, manage, and promote change to create a leadership position personally and professionally" (Rideout, 2011, p. 14).

- **Cultural Intelligence:** "An outsider's seemingly natural ability to interpret someone's unfamiliar and ambiguous gestures the way that person's compatriots would" (Earley & Mosakowski, 2004, p. 140).

- **Emotional Intelligence:** The leader's ability to become cognizant of his or her emotions and moods, including those of other stakeholders in the external environment (George, 2000).

Appendix D

Case Study Significant Events

- **Early 1980s**—Hanley shoe based in Bangor merged with Tatsu manufacturing, a South Korean shoe manufacturer. Hanley employed 2200 workers. By 1997 all Hanley manufacturing shifted to foreign markets.

- **November 1986**—Donald attends the world shoe expo in Houston, TX for the first time. Donald marvels at the unique styles coming from foreign markets. Donald's father, Ralph, declares during the show that cheap foreign imports will never replace quality American-made shoes. Donald ponders how this may influence Southeast Shoe.

- **May 1989**—Donald's grandfather, Charles Glidden, dies at 84.

- **January, 1994**—NAFTA implemented opening the door to free trade with Canada, and Mexico

- **November 1996**—Donald attends the world shoe expo in New York City. Donald can see a vast difference in the selection of shoes; nearly all are foreign imports. Donald meets Norman Douglas from Douglas Shoe, a local competitor, for dinner during the show. Donald and Norman grew up together and have been friends for many years. Norman laments that things are changing quickly, and he does not know how much longer his family can hold on before selling out. The tone of the conversation is much different than

Donald expects. Norman is usually upbeat, and always has a can-do attitude. Donald wonders if Norman has had too much to drink.

- **May 1997** – Hanley Shoe officially closes manufacturing operations in Maine. Hanley is now fully owned by Tatsu. Tatsu moves all sales and office operations to their U.S. home office in Richmond, VA.

- **June 1998**—The last competitor in the local market, Douglas Shoe, closes. The company employed nearly 500 workers in Gardiner, Augusta, and Winslow, Maine. Southeast Shoe hired over 200 of the workers. Besides Southeast Shoe, the only shoe companies left in Maine are McDonough Goods based in Hampton and Murphy Manufacturing in Portland.

- **April 2001**—Ralph Glidden Jr. retires from Southeast Shoe. Donald Glidden is named CEO at 38.

Appendix E

Case Study Answer Key

The following answer key is meant as a guide to offer a basis for creating dialogue with students. Classroom dialogue may reveal a rich array of solutions and viewpoints beyond the scope or capabilities of this answer key.

1. Using the LQ³ model (see *Figure 1*) as a guide, identify the change stressors creating the decision-making process for Donald.

   Donald is experiencing change caused by various systems and resulting change forces. The primary systems creating change are the free trade system and the economic environment.

   a) Free trade (system)+Competition (change force)—Examples such as NAFTA and the increase in foreign imports points to the free trade system creating competitive change forces influencing Southeast and Donald's decision-making process.

   b) Free trade (system)+Supply chain (change force)—This creates the need for Donald to expand the supply chain, and look for new suppliers who can enhance the company's competitive edge.

   c) Economic (system)+Financial (change force)—The lackluster economy is precipitating the financial malaise, and causing the company to change, such as establishing new banking relationships.

   d) Economic (system)+Free trade (systems)+Fear (change force)—Donald knows if he does not adapt quickly the company will fail.

2. Using the definitions provided in Appendix C, how do change leadership, cultural, and emotional intelligence play a role in Donald's decision-making process?

   a) Change leadership intelligence—Change leadership intelligence will play a key role in the course of action Donald decides to take. Donald's ability to identify short and long-term future change can positively or negatively influence his decision. For instance, if Donald believes new government regulations will favor free trade; he may decide to move production offshore.

   b) Cultural intelligence—Donald's cultural intelligence will play a significant role in decision making because in each option Donald is forced to consider foreign or unknown cultures. If Donald decides to move production offshore he must learn to adapt to cultures that may be non-American. Likewise, if he decides to retool or idle one or more plants he must show his savvy when dealing with local cultures (employees and local community), and those in other fields such as banking.

   c) Emotional intelligence—In any of the decision options, Donald must step outside his comfort zone and establish new relationships. Donald's emotional intelligence or how well he can feel comfortable stepping outside this zone will determine his success or failure leading the company.

3. Do you think Donald has high or low change leadership, cultural, and emotional intelligence? Why?

The likely answer is a mixture of high and low:

a) Change Leadership Intelligence=High to low—Donald began questioning early in his career the influence of foreign imports on Southeast Shoe, but did little to position the company to manage or use this change effectively.

b) Cultural Intelligence=High to low—Donald's cultural intelligence may be considered high for his local community, such as with workers and business associates. Conversely, when dealing with the unknown, such as foreign markets, Donald has low cultural intelligence.

c) Emotional Intelligence=High to low—Similar to cultural intelligence Donald has a comfort zone. When stepping outside this zone, it is apparent Donald lacks confidence because of inexperience.

4. What biases are evident in Donald's decision-making process, and can you explain the relationship between the intelligences?

Donald has obvious biases resulting from his life experiences. Although Donald is privileged compared with others in his community, he lives an isolated life. Donald's change leadership, cultural, and emotional intelligences are based on these life experiences. Another example comes from Donald's belief and value system taught by his grandfather. This belief system stymied Donald's growth.

The intelligences show a clear inter-relationship, working asynchronously, and synchronously influencing Donald's decision-making process. The intelligences influence each other by creating positive and negative challenges for Donald. For instance, if Donald has strong change leadership intelligence and recognizes the need to adapt to a situation but lacks the emotional intelligence to feel confident to make the decision the opportunity is hindered.

5. How do you think Donald's decision-making capabilities are enhanced or hindered by his intelligences?

See question four.

6. What could Donald do to enhance his intelligences and decision-making capabilities?

For Donald, the answer may center on gaining experience. By allowing himself to step outside his comfort zone, Donald will heighten his awareness and the corresponding intelligences. The crux of this heightened awareness is education. Knowledge is a result of the learning process. For Donald to enhance his intelligences he must expose himself to new environments that will provide the stimulus for education.

Appendix F

Suggested Readings

Anonymous. (2009). Good leaders making bad decisions? *The Journal of Applied Christian Leadership, 3*(2), 8.

Chrusciel, D. (2006). Considerations of emotional intelligence (EI) in dealing with change decision management. *Management Decision, 44*(5), 644.

Collins, C. (2001). Developing critical consciousness: a personal reflection. *The Canadian Journal for the Study of Adult Education, 15*(1), 88.

Crowne, K. A. (2009). The relationships among social intelligence, emotional intelligence and cultural intelligence. *Organization Management Journal, 6*(3), 148-163. doi: 10.1057/omj.2009.20

Donham, J. (2010). Creating personal learning through self-assessment. *Teacher Librarian, 37*(3), 14-14-21.

Folaron, J. (2005). The human side of change leadership. *Quality Progress, 38*(4), 39-43.

Fowlie, J., & Wood, M. (2009). The emotional impact of leaders' behaviours. *Journal of European Industrial Training, 33*(6), 559. doi: 10.1108/03090590910974428

Goleman, D. (2000). Leadership that gets results. *Harvard Business Review, 78*(2), 78-90.

Graetz, F. (2000). Strategic change leadership. *Management Decision, 38*(8).

Griffer, M. R., & Perlis, S. M. (2007). Developing cultural intelligence in preservice speech-language pathologists and educators. *Communication Disorders Quarterly, 29*(1), 28. doi: 10.1177/1525740107312546

Karp, T. (2006). Transforming organisations for organic growth: The DNA of change leadership. *Journal of Change Management, 6*(1), 3-20. doi: 10.1080/14697010600565186

Katzenbach, J. R. (1996). New roads to job opportunity: From middle manager to real change leader. *Strategy & Leadership, 24*(4).

Kyriacou, D. N. (2004). Evidence-based medical decision making: Deductive versus inductive logical thinking. *Academic Emergency Medicine, 11*(6), 670-670-671.

Maccoby, M. (2010). Learn change leadership from two great teachers. *Research Technology Management, 53*(2), 68.

Marine, A., & Riley, P. (1995). Creating a culture of change. *Hospital materiel management quarterly, 16*(4), 30.

McDonald, J. M. (2000). Managing rapid change: From theory to practice: An invited article. *Southern Business Review, 25*(2), 28.

McGivern, M. H. (1998). Vision driven organizations: A case study in applied change. *Futurics, 22*(3/4), 1-1-15.

McGrath, R., & MacMillan, I. (2009). How to rethink your business during uncertainty. *MIT Sloan Management Review, 50*(3), 25.

Mockler, R. J. (1968). The systems approach to business organization and decision making. *California Management Review, 11*(2), 53-58.

Murray, A. J., & Greenes, K. A. (2006). New leadership strategies for the enterprise of the future. *VINE, 36*(4), 358. doi: 10.1108/03055720610716629

Oudan, R. (2010). Strategic decision making in the emerging field of E-commerce. *International Journal of Management and Information Systems, 14*(2), 19.

Pilárik, L., & Sarmány-Schuller, I. (2009). Emotional intelligence and decision making of female students of social work in the Iowa gambling task. *Studia Psychologia, 51*(4), 319.

Pluta, P. (2010). Being proactive may be difficult. *Journal of GXP Compliance, 14*(3), 4.

Reid, J., & Crisp, D. (2007). The talent challenge: Creating a culture to recruit, engage and retain the best. *Ivey Business Journal Online.*

Robertson, S. (2007). Got EQ? Increasing cultural and clinical competence through emotional intelligence. *Communication Disorders Quarterly, 29*(1), 14. doi: 10.1177/1525740108314864

Rogers, P., & Meehan, P. (2007). Building a winning culture. *Business Strategy Series, 8*(4), 254. doi: 10.1108/17515630710684420

Schwarber, P. D. (2005). Leaders and the decision-making process. *Management Decision, 43*(7/8), 1086. doi: 10.1108/00251740510610099

Skarzauskiene, A. (2010). Managing complexity: systems thinking as a catalyst of the organization performance. *Measuring business excellence, 14*(4), 49. doi: 10.1108/13683041011093758

Thomas, D. C. (2006). Domain and development of cultural intelligence: The importance of mindfulness. *Group & Organization Management, 31*(1), 78. doi: 10.1177/1059601105275266

Triandis, H. C. (2006). Cultural intelligence in organizations. *Group & Organization Management, 31*(1), 20. doi: 10.1177/1059601105275253

White, H., & Lean, E. (2008). The impact of perceived leader integrity on subordinates in a work team environment. *Journal of Business Ethics, 81*(4), 765.

Appendix G

Download Links

Evolution Strategists Press is proud to offer complimentary download links for the sample case study and PowerPoint presentations to facilitate classroom instruction.

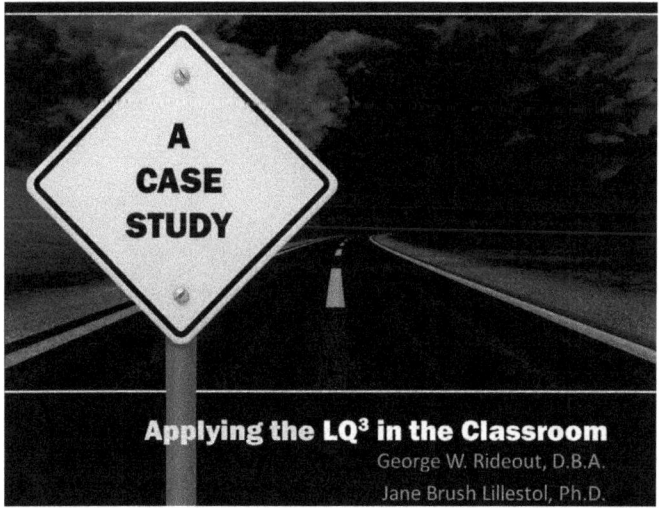

For your free links, please send an email to info@evolutionstrategists.com. When sending your email, please note in the subject line "LQ3 Download Links." You will receive a website link and password. The password will be good for 30 days. Please note, downloads are limited to one copy. By requesting and downloading materials, you agree that all materials downloaded are for your own use, may be used in your personal classroom instruction, and may not be distributed or copied without the consent of Evolution Strategists Press.

About the Authors

George W. Rideout, D.B.A.

George W. Rideout, D.B.A., is a principal for Evolution Strategists LLC, and executive director of the Change Leadership Intelligence (CLQ) Institute. Dr. Rideout holds an MBA and numerous professional certifications including the certified six sigma black belt (CSSBB). He has more than 16 years' experience in sales and management, leading sales teams in the United States and Canada. Dr. Rideout is a member of various professional associations including the Association of Leadership Educators (ALE), the Institute of Management Consultants (IMC), and the International Leadership Association (ILA). His research interests include change leadership, decision making, leadership studies, multiple intelligences, and systems theories.

*****

Jane Brush Lillestol, Ph.D.

Jane Brush Lillestol, Ph.D., is a faculty member at the University Of Phoenix School Of Advanced Studies and faculty emerita and former dean and vice president at Syracuse University. Dr. Lillestol received her Ph.D. from the University of Minnesota. She is presently recognized in *Who's Who in America*, *Who's Who of American Women*, and *International Who's Who of Professional and Business Women*.

www.ingramcontent.com/pod-product-compliance
Lightning Source LLC
Chambersburg PA
CBHW060645210326
41520CB00010B/1751